How to be a little
Princess

This is a Parragon Book
First published in 2002

Parragon
Queen Street House, 4 Queen Street,
Bath, BA1 1HE, UK

Designed by Caroline Reeves
and Kilnwood Graphics

Printed and bound in China
ISBN 0 75258 707 2

How to be a little
Princess

p

Written by Caroline Repchuk • Illustrated by Kim Blundell

Once upon a time...

... there was a young girl called Poppy, who was busy mucking out the stables where she worked. She was too busy to notice a twinkling ball of light appear behind her. An adventure was about to begin that would change her life forever!

"Phew! What an awful stink!"
With a fizz of stars, a fairy
appeared, holding her nose with
a dainty hand.

"Hello Poppy. I'm your Fairy
Godmother, here to make your
dreams come true!" said the fairy.

"You mean, I'm going to win the
gymkhana?" cried Poppy.

"No dear, you're going to win
the heart of a handsome prince,
although I think I've got my work
cut out!" said the fairy, looking at
Poppy's messy clothes in disgust.
"Come on, there's no time to lose!"

Pretty as a Princess

With a wave of her magic wand, and a sprinkling of fairy dust, Poppy's Fairy Godmother set about transforming her at once. Soon she was kitted out from the top of her tiara to the tips of her glass slippers like a true fairytale princess.

Lesson One – Get the Look!

Join Poppy, and put on a pretty party dress, or dig in your dressing-up box and use your imagination! Add some tinsel for a sparkly sash, the lovely tiara from your princess pack, and soon you too will be pretty as a princess!

Beauty Tips

Though beauty may be just skin deep,
   Always remember your beauty sleep!

"These potions are just what you need to get rid of the smell of the stables," the Fairy Godmother said to Poppy. "And they will soften up those hard-working hands!"

Silky Soft

Soften dry or chapped hands by soaking in a bowl of warm olive oil for ten minutes. Wipe off the extra oil with a tissue, and your hands will be soft as silk!

Heaven Scent

Put some dried herbs and flowers (such as lavender and rose petals) into a small muslin bag, and secure the top with an elastic band.

Dried herbs and flowers
Muslin bag
Elastic band
Ribbon

Tie some ribbon around to decorate. Hang the bag over the hot water tap on your bath, so the water runs through it as the bath fills. Sure to make you smell heavenly!

9

Past Princesses

"Now for a history lesson, dear," said the Fairy Godmother. Poppy sat and listened, as her Fairy Godmother filled her in on some of the famous princesses in whose dainty footsteps she was to follow:

Snow White

A beautiful princess with skin as white as snow. She lived in the forest with seven dwarves, to escape her wicked stepmother, who tried to choke her with a poisoned apple. A handsome prince revived her, they got married, and lived happily ever after.

Cinderella

A lovely girl, treated as a servant by her evil stepmother and ugly stepsisters. Transformed by her Fairy Godmother into a beautiful princess, she went to a ball and won the heart of the prince, who searched the land to find her again, and married her at once!

Sleeping Beauty

A charming princess, who slept for a hundred years after pricking her finger on a spindle, because of a spell put on her by a wicked fairy. Kissed awake by a handsome prince, whom she married and lived with happily ever after.

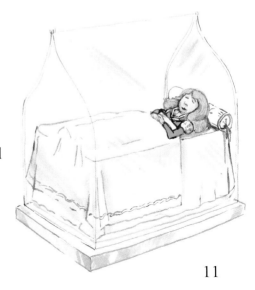

Dangers and Dragons

"It's not all hearts and flowers being a princess," said the Fairy Godmother, "what with dragons carrying you off, witches locking you up, and evil stepmothers trying to bump you off. Still forewarned is forearmed!"

Bad Fairies

Grumpy old fairies, who've been forgotten about. Prone to popping up when least expected and casting bad spells.

Dragons

Large scaly fire-breathing monsters, who love princesses for breakfast. Will pounce when you are least expecting it and carry you off.

Wicked Witches

Nasty old hags, usually living in cottages deep in
the woods. Fond of removing young princesses from
happy homes and locking them in towers. Will offer
all kinds of tempting goodies in order to fatten you up
for the pot!

Vital Accessories

Poppy was beginning to wonder whether this whole princess business was worth the trouble, when her Fairy Godmother handed her an invitation:

You are invited to a Grand Ball to be held in the ballroom at the Royal Palace on Saturday night.

Time: 8 till late
From: Prince Charming

Poppy's heart skipped a beat – how could she resist? With a wave of her Fairy Godmother's wand, some mice became footmen, a bucket became a carriage, and her old donkey became a silver charger! Poppy put on her dancing shoes, and prepared to party!

You Shall Go to the Ball!

In true fairytale tradition Poppy danced all night and captured the prince's heart, before disappearing at midnight, leaving one glass slipper behind. But before the prince came looking for her, she had a lot to consider...

You Have to Kiss a Lot of Frogs...

"Let me remind you of the story of the Frog Prince, Poppy," said her Fairy Godmother. "A young princess was playing with her golden ball in the palace garden, when she dropped it in the pond. A helpful frog retrieved it, on a promise of eating, drinking and sleeping with the princess at the palace.

That night the frog turned up and the king made her keep her promise. To her delight, the frog turned into a prince and asked her to marry him!"

"I remember that story," said Poppy. "But what's the point?"

"The point is," said the Fairy Godmother, "is your prince really charming, or just a frog? Take a look at this checklist, and find out!"

CHECKLIST

Handsome
Fit and Trim
Charming
Funny
Romantic
Smart
Brave

19

Wedding Bells?

Now, the prince soon came looking for Poppy,
Who at once went all giggly and soppy,
He went down on one knee,
And said, "Please marry me!"
And gave her a kiss, wet and sloppy!

Poppy sank to her chair in a swoon,
And asked, "Don't you think it's too soon?"
Said the prince, "Not for me,
I'm in love, can't you see?
Marry me, and I'll give you the moon!"

Said Poppy, "I won't make you guess,
For you sure know just how to impress,
So don't dally, don't linger,
Put a ring on my finger,
And make me a little princess!"

21

The Way to a Prince's Heart...

Of course, her Fairy Godmother was delighted with the news. "Most princes have a sweet tooth," she advised. "It's all that feasting they grow up with. These cookies are sure to be a hit!"

Love Heart Cookies

You will need:
25g (1oz) muscovado sugar
50g (2oz) margarine
75g (3oz) plain wholemeal flour
silver balls to decorate
tube of icing for writing

1. Beat the sugar and margarine until light and fluffy.

2. Add the flour and mix until the mixture binds together.

3. Turn onto a floured surface and knead until smooth. Roll out thinly, then cut out using a heart-shaped cutter.

4. Decorate around the edges with silver balls, then bake in a preheated oven, 170°c/325°F/Gas Mark 3, for 15 mins. Leave to cool on the baking sheet.

5. Write on your own message of love with the tube of icing!

Top Tip:
Find a grown-up to help you with the hot bits – a princess shouldn't do all her own work!

Meet the Family

All good fairytales must have them, and this one is no exception! Before Poppy weds her prince, she finds out just what kind of family tree she'll be climbing!

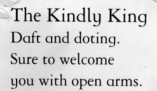

The Kindly King
Daft and doting.
Sure to welcome
you with open arms.

The Kid Brother
Impossible to imagine this one will grow into anything other than a frog! Tell the slimy little tadpole to crawl back under his lilypad!

The Wicked Stepmother

She may slip the odd pea under your mattress when you're not expecting it. And avoid looking in her magic mirror at any time!

The Ugly Sisters

Mean and selfish. Will poke fun at every opportunity, and treat you like a servant.

The Handsome Prince

Hard to believe he comes from such a dreadful family, but no-one's perfect!

A Perfect Princess

"Well, Poppy, the time has come to marry
the prince and become a princess!" said
Poppy's Fairy Godmother. "And to be sure
you're ready, I've set a little test for you."

**1. A prince arrives holding
a glass slipper. Do you:**
a. Slip your foot daintily into it
and look hopeful.
b. Drop it, but offer to pay for
the damage.
c. Tell him you prefer your wellies.

**2. A prince kisses you awake after
a hundred year sleep. Do you:**
a. Fall instantly in love and
agree to marry him.
b. Tell him his breath is smelly!
c. Roll over and go back to sleep.

3. A frog turns up at your door demanding dinner. Do you:

a. Wine and dine him, before settling him on your pillow.

b. Give him a plate of leftovers and a bed in the bathtub.

c. Threaten to put frog's legs on the menu if he doesn't hop it!

4. Your Fairy Godmother helps find the prince of your dreams. Do you:

a. Grant whatever she wishes.

b. Buy her a retirement cottage.

c. Tell her not to interfere in your love life!

Mostly a's: Well done. You will make a perfect princess!

Mostly b's: Your heart's in the right place, but you've a lot to learn!

Mostly c's: You're bad enough to make the ugly sisters look promising! (Poppy passed the test with full marks! Did you?)

A Fairytale Wedding

Poppy's big day finally arrived, and as she swept down the aisle in her dazzling dress there was not a single dry eye in the house!

Invitation

You are cordially invited to the wedding of Poppy and Prince Charming on Saturday at 2pm at the Royal Palace followed by a Banquet and dancing in the Glass Ballroom

Ideal Home

And so, Poppy married her prince, and they set
up home in their very own fairytale palace, which had
everything a princess could wish for. Only, most often
Princess Poppy could be found in the place she loved best,
doing the thing she loved most of all — helping the prince
with his horses down at the stables!

"After everything I've taught you!" sighed Poppy's Fairy
Godmother, looking at her messy clothes with a smile!

And they all lived happily ever after!

The End